W9-CHP-933

VERSUS

SERENA WILLIAMS

VS.

BILLIE JEAN KING

BY ALEX MONNIG

SportsZone

An Imprint of Abdo Publishing
abdopublishing.com

abdopublishing.com

Published by Abdo Publishing, a division of ABDO, PO Box 398166, Minneapolis, Minnesota 55439. Copyright © 2018 by Abdo Consulting Group, Inc. International copyrights reserved in all countries. No part of this book may be reproduced in any form without written permission from the publisher. SportsZone™ is a trademark and logo of Abdo Publishing.

Printed in the United States of America, North Mankato, Minnesota
102017
012018

THIS BOOK CONTAINS RECYCLED MATERIALS

Cover Photos: Kathy Willens/AP Images, right; Julian Finney/Getty Images Sport/Getty Images, left
Interior Photos: Jason Heidrich/Icon Sportswire/Newscom, 4–5 (left); Tony Duffy/Getty Images Sport/Getty Images, 4–5 (right); John Cordes/Icon Sportswire/Newscom, 6–7; Jay Talbott/Corbis/Icon SMI/Newscom, 8; Bettmann/Getty Images, 9, 18–19; AP Images, 10, 15, 16, 20, 24–25, 26, 27; Alberto E. Tamargo/Sipa USA/Newscom, 12–13; Adam Davis/Icon SMI/Newscom, 14; John Angelillo/UPI/Newscom, 21, 22; Anja Niedringhaus/AP Images, 28

Editor: Patrick Donnelly
Series Designer: Sarah Winkler

Publisher's Cataloging-in-Publication Data
Names: Monnig, Alex, author.
Title: Serena Williams vs. Billie Jean King / by Alex Monnig.
Other titles: Serena Williams versus Billie Jean King
Description: Minneapolis, Minnesota : Abdo Publishing, 2018. | Series: Versus | Includes online resources and index.
Identifiers: LCCN 2017946925 | ISBN 9781532113574 (lib.bdg.) | ISBN 9781532152450 (ebook)
Subjects: LCSH: Tennis players--Juvenile literature. | Tennis--Records--Juvenile literature. | Sports--History--Juvenile literature.
Classification: DDC 796.342--dc23
LC record available at https://lccn.loc.gov/2017946925

TABLE OF CONTENTS

INTRODUCTION

Billie Jean King and Serena Williams are two of the best to ever set foot on a tennis court. Both dominated their eras, though they did so in different ways. King's technical prowess made her one of the sport's most popular stars in the 1960s and '70s. But Williams took an alternate route to the pinnacle of tennis, setting an Open Era record with 23 Grand Slam singles titles through 2017.

Who's better? It's an argument without a right or wrong answer. We'll tell their stories and lay out the facts.

SERENA OR BILLIE JEAN? YOU DECIDE!

Serena Williams has used her big serve to become one of the top women's tennis players of all time.

CHAPTER 1

SERVING

Serena Williams might be the most powerful player in the history of women's tennis. Her amazing strength especially helps her dominate opponents with her serve.

For proof, look no further than the final of the 2013 French Open. Williams crushed three aces past Maria Sharapova in the last game to win the title. The first was 118 miles per hour (190 km/h). The second was 121 mph (195 km/h).

The third ace was a thing of beauty. Williams tossed the ball up on match point. She reached high and slammed downward with her racket. The ball sizzled over the net and down the T at a flaming 123 mph (198 km/h). It flew by Sharapova so quickly she did not even bother reaching for it. The title belonged to Williams.

Williams's outstanding serve starts with a consistent toss. Then she leans forward and bends her legs to load up the considerable energy she has in her powerful frame. She explodes upward,

7

Williams gets full extension to maximize the power behind her serve.

sending the power in her legs up through her body to her right elbow. It straightens as she swings to hit the ball at as high a point overhead as possible.

The consistency of this motion allows Williams to make contact with the ball at virtually the same spot each time she serves. That makes it harder to tell which type of serve is coming. Opponents are left to guess if they have to deal with a hard flat serve, a kick serve that bounces away from them, or a slice down the T.

This process delivers dependable results time and time again. Williams won Wimbledon in 2016 and led the tournament with 74 aces. Her semifinal opponent, Elena Vesnina, was the next closest player with 31. And Williams ranked in the top two in aces in Women's Tennis Association (WTA) tour events each year from 2012 to 2016.

Billie Jean King didn't have a powerful serve, but her accurate placement kept her opponents on the run.

Williams really let it rip in a match at the 2013 Australian Open, when she belted a serve at 128.6 mph (207 km/h). That is the third-fastest recorded serve in women's tennis history.

Billie Jean King did not have the luxury of Williams's height or strength. Her shorter stature meant she had to rely on her technique to generate serving power. In 1964, trying to capture the No. 1 ranking in the world, King went to Australia where former tennis star Mervyn Rose helped her perfect her serve. While King was not particularly known for racking up aces, she was a master at using her serve to force opponents into returns that she could easily handle with her unparalleled volley.

King used her serve to finish off Chris Evert in the 1973 Wimbledon final.

10

MEET THE PLAYERS

BILLIE JEAN KING

- Born November 22, 1943, in Long Beach, California
- 5 feet, 4½ inches/134 pounds
- Home today: New York City

SERENA WILLIAMS

- Born September 26, 1981, in Saginaw, Michigan
- 5 feet, 9 inches/155 pounds
- Home today: Palm Beach Gardens, Florida

Rose taught King to get the most out of her limited height by tossing the ball higher and stretching her racket toward it. This generated more power and created better serving angles that made for tougher returns.

For much of her career, King relied on a slicing serve that featured spin to keep returners from getting too comfortable. It spun to the side and dragged her opponents away from the court. This led to weaker returns that were perfect for King to capitalize on with her masterful volley.

The effectiveness of her crosscourt serve was on display at the 1973 Wimbledon final. King used this tactic to win the last four points of the match against Chris Evert. Match point was a particularly good example. King whipped the ball over the net with her serve. The ball hit the ground and bounced sharply to Evert's right. Evert tried to return the ball with a simple forehand. But the ball sailed wide, the spin of the serve too much for Evert to control.

Williams relies on balance to set up her deadly forehand.

CHAPTER 2

FOREHAND

If a player can return Williams's vicious serve, then she has to be ready for a hard, flat forehand rocketing back over the net. The forehand is one of the most common strokes in tennis. On the forehand, players hit the ball on the side of their dominant hand. Most players hit this shot harder than they hit their backhand.

Williams's forehand is a throwback to the players of years past. She usually uses a classic style in which the racket passes across the front of her body and wraps around her left shoulder. This is a stark contrast to the "copter finish" that has become popular. In this method, players whip the racket around their heads like the rotors of a helicopter. The motion finishes with the racket on the same side of the body where they made contact with the ball. Williams sometimes mixes in the copter finish to apply a different spin on the ball.

Williams explodes up and through the ball to add power to her forehand strokes.

But she doesn't always rely on such spin. Her favorite forehand is a hard, flat, and deep crosscourt winner.

As with her serve, Williams's forehand requires strength from parts of her body beyond her right arm. She sets a powerful foundation angled slightly toward her right side. Her left foot is a bit in front of her right foot. Her legs are spread approximately shoulder-width apart to form a solid base from which to attack.

As the ball heads toward her, she stretches her left arm in front of her body and raises her racket as she bends her right arm. When the ball passes across the front of her body, she boosts power from her legs and explodes on an upward trajectory through the ball, sending it scorching across the net. The racket ends outside her opposite shoulder.

She hit one of her most memorable forehands at the end of the 2015 French Open. Opponent Lucie Šafářová served deep to Williams's forehand side. Williams took one short step to her right, set her strong base, and whipped the racket through the ball. The crosscourt shot thundered across the net.

Šafářová was on the same side of the court as Williams's shot. But it was too powerful to handle. All she could do was attempt a feeble backhand that landed a few feet in front of her. Williams just needed one step, her ferocious strength,

King displays her forehand form at Wimbledon in 1962.

15

and flawless mechanics to return the serve of one of the best players in the world with her elite forehand.

King, on the other hand, did not rely on her forehand as much as Williams does now. King grew up learning how to hit a forehand improperly. Even as she progressed through the ranks in her march toward the top, she had a looping action on her backswing that made the stroke slow to develop.

King learned to use her whole body to generate power on her forehand.

PROFESSIONAL SUCCESS

BILLIE JEAN KING

- Years active: 1959–84
- Tournaments won: 168 (Open Era, post-1967)
- Grand Slam singles titles: 12 (1 Australian Open, 1 French Open, 6 Wimbledon, 4 US Open)

SERENA WILLIAMS

- Years active: 1995–present
- Tournaments won: 72 (through 2017)
- Grand Slam singles titles: 23 (7 Australian Open, 3 French Open, 7 Wimbledon, 6 US Open)

But just as her serve improved under Rose's instruction, her forehand did, too. Instead of loading up on her backswing so much, King shortened it. He also advised her to use a tighter grip on her racket and to not tilt the head of the racket behind her wrist.

From there she kept working, constantly improving the turning of her hips and shoulders to provide the torque necessary for an effective forehand. Even though her serves and volleys were always considered the stronger points of her game, King's ability to hone her ground strokes helped her become one of the best all-around players ever.

While it was still often cited as the weakest part of her game, King worked at her forehand until it measured up to the rest of her outstanding tennis arsenal.

King began her backhand strokes with her racket held high.

CHAPTER 3

BACKHAND

The backhand does not usually generate as much power as the forehand, but it can still be a deadly shot. Williams hits winners with her backhand. King didn't do that often, but she used hers to set up her dominant net game.

King's backhand was not powerful. She used a traditional one-handed backhand, often playing it from deeper in the court. King started with her racket high on her backswing. Then, with a looping motion almost in the shape of a U, she chopped down on the ball. Instead of hitting it straight and hard, the slice created backspin.

The shot wouldn't break any speed records. But King could place it wonderfully. The slower, floating ball also gave her time to break to the net, where she could set up to go to work on the volley, considered by most to be her best skill. Often she would blend

King chopped down on the ball on her backhand to create extreme backspin.

her follow-through with a charge to the net, seamlessly starting her sprint to the forecourt as she chopped down on the ball.

The final point of the 1975 Wimbledon tournament left viewers with a great example of this memorable shot. Evonne Goolagong Cawley served to King's backhand side. King raised her racket and sliced under the ball, sending it floating with backspin over the net. As she finished her stroke, King, in one fluid motion, charged toward the net. Goolagong Cawley tried to hit a backhand shot past King's forehand. But King easily volleyed it home to win. The winning point was set up by her supreme backhand technique.

As with her other strokes, Williams's strength allows her to zip backhands all over the court. But her technique plays a big role in that shot's success. Williams uses a wide stance when she launches a backhand assault. Many players start their one-handed backhand stroke with their shoulders perpendicular to the net. But Williams faces the net, her shoulders parallel to the baseline, and uses a two-handed backhand.

Williams squares her shoulders to the net as she sets up for her two-handed backhand.

This technique is a departure from the traditional method that has dominated the game for years. Her dominant hand, her right, is below her left hand, and she channels her body's strength through her left arm as her dominant hand guides the shot. She makes sure to give herself enough room to extend her limbs for maximum power.

This form requires a bit more strength to muscle the ball over the net. That's not an issue for Williams. Her power was apparent even before she became one of the all-time greats. Williams's backhand played a big part in putting the finishing touches on her first major victory, the 1999 US Open. Williams boomed one of her patented hard serves over the net at Martina Hingis. Hingis returned the serve deep into Williams's side of the court, forcing her onto her heels. Williams couldn't

Williams uses her left hand on top to guide her backhand strokes.

22

BILLIE JEAN KING

- First Grand Slam singles title: 1966 Wimbledon
- Career highlight: King defeated Bobby Riggs in the "Battle of the Sexes" in 1973.
- Awards won: 1972 *Sports Illustrated* Sportsperson of the Year; inducted into the International Tennis Hall of Fame in 1987; 1999 Arthur Ashe Courage Award
- Record in Grand Slam finals (including doubles): 39–26

SERENA WILLIAMS

- First Grand Slam singles title: 1999 US Open
- Career highlight: Williams won the 2017 Australian Open to set an Open Era record with her 23rd Grand Slam singles title.
- Awards won: Four-time Associated Press Women's Athlete of the Year; *Sports Illustrated* Best Female Athlete of the Decade in 2009
- Grand Slam record against her sister Venus: 6–2

get enough separation from the ball to fully extend her arms and use all her power. And her weight was still taking her backward. But she still crushed the ball back over the net.

Hingis returned again, but this time Williams was able to set her feet and wallop the ball. Hingis got to it but hit it long, giving Williams her first Grand Slam singles win. She put the match away with two effective ground strokes, both backhands.

King charged the net often to keep her opponents on the run with her strong volley game.

CHAPTER 4

VOLLEYING

A good volley can catch opponents off guard and be a quick and easy way to win points. Williams is great at rushing to the net. But King might have been the best ever. She did not try to overpower others with her volley; she tried to win points with accuracy and touch. When in doubt, King rushed to the net. She was confident enough to trust her amazing volley placement to put her opponents under pressure. They often had to change their shots to try to beat King's secret weapon.

King's forehand volley was good. But her backhand volley was even better. Some writers at the time thought she had the best backhand volley in tennis, male or female. Her incredible footwork and body control allowed her to get in perfect position to make the shot.

King called upon her volleying skills in the 1971 US Open final against Rosemary Casals. King faced a tiebreaker in the

King shows off her forehand volley against Chris Evert at the 1971 US Open.

second set. The first player to win five points and lead by two would win the set.

King led 4–2 as she served. She immediately charged the net, as she was known to do. Casals returned the serve to the middle of the court. Without missing a beat on her charge, King bent down low and executed a perfect backhand volley to the far left corner of Casals's court. Casals sprinted over and lobbed the ball over King's head. But King wasn't rattled. She ran back a few steps, reached up, and slammed a forehand volley winner to take the title.

Like King in her prime, Williams has few holes in her game. She has amazing court coverage and is no slouch when it comes to playing at the net. Volleying is an important skill in doubles tennis. That's where Williams has had a lot of success. She had won 14 Grand Slam doubles titles through 2017, all with her sister Venus as her partner.

When setting up her volleys, Williams rushes to the net to get set, opening her body to better control the shot. She also makes sure to keep her head down, watching the ball all the way into her racket.

Williams relies on speed and quick reactions to charge the net.

27

Williams does not have to rely on the volley quite as much. She can use her strong ground strokes to smash the ball past her opponents instead. But that doesn't mean she's afraid to charge the net when she needs to. And she needed to in the 2016 Wimbledon final against Angelique Kerber.

Williams was serving for her 22nd Grand Slam singles title. Kerber's return was short, forcing Williams to charge to the net. Kerber's next shot was a hard, crosscourt laser to Williams's backhand side. But Williams defused the situation with a slicing backhand volley. Her delicate touch sent the ball floating to the baseline. Kerber scrambled to it and hit a soft forehand. One simple forehand volley later and Williams had won yet another Grand Slam title.

Williams lunges for a backhand volley at Wimbledon in 2010.

28

BILLIE JEAN KING

- Important records: 20 Wimbledon titles (6 singles, 10 doubles, 4 mixed doubles), tied for most ever with Martina Navratilova; first sportswoman to win $100,000 in a year

- Key rivals: Margaret Court, Evonne Goolagong Cawley

- Off-court accomplishments: Was president of the WTA; founded *Women's Sports Magazine* and the Women's Sports Foundation; awarded the Presidential Medal of Freedom in 2009

"Champions keep playing until they get it right."

—Billie Jean King

SERENA WILLIAMS

- Important records: 23 Grand Slam singles titles; oldest player to win a Grand Slam singles title

- Key rivals: Venus Williams, Maria Sharapova

- Off-court accomplishments: Launched her own clothing line, Aneres; started the Serena Williams Fund and helped create the Williams Sisters Fund

"I just never give up. I fight to the end. You can't go out and say, 'I want a bag of never-say-die spirit.' It's not for sale. It has to be innate."

—Serena Williams

More often than not, Williams can get away with overpowering her opponents. But King did not have such a muscular frame. She relied on her swift and nimble footwork and touch. That helped make King the queen of the volley.

Glossary

ACE
A serve that cannot be returned, earning a point for the server.

BASELINE
The line at each end of a tennis court.

COURT COVERAGE
The ability to move quickly to reach an opponent's shots.

DOUBLES
A match played between two teams of two players.

GRAND SLAM
The four most prestigious events in tennis—the Australian Open, the French Open, Wimbledon, and the US Open.

KICK SERVE
A serve that spins away from the player receiving the serve after it bounces.

OPEN ERA
The time when professional players were allowed to play in Grand Slam tournaments; before 1968 only amateur players could enter those events.

SLICE
A stroke that uses spin to cause the ball to bounce low or backwards.

THE T
The point where the center line and the service line intersect, forming the shape of a T.

VOLLEY
Returning the ball before it hits the ground.

WINNER
A shot that the opposing player cannot reach, winning the point.

ONLINE RESOURCES

Booklinks
NONFICTION NETWORK
FREE! ONLINE NONFICTION RESOURCES

To learn more about great tennis players, visit abdobooklinks.com. These links are routinely monitored and updated to provide the most current information available.

MORE INFORMATION

BOOKS

Gitlin, Marty. *Billie Jean King: Tennis Star & Social Activist*. Minneapolis, MN: Abdo Publishing, 2011.

Ignotofsky, Rachel. *Women in Sports: 50 Fearless Athletes Who Played to Win*. New York: Ten Speed Press, 2017.

Shepherd, Jodie. *Serena Williams: A Champion on and off the Court*. New York: Children's Press, 2017.

INDEX

ABOUT THE AUTHOR

Alex Monnig is a freelance journalist from St. Louis, Missouri, who now lives in Sydney, Australia. He graduated with his master's degree from the University of Missouri in 2010. He has covered sporting events around the world and written more than 20 children's books.